THE NEED TO KNOW LIBRARY™

EVERYTHING YOU NEED TO KNOW ABOUT

ALCOHOLISM

ERIN PACK AND PHILIP WOLNY

Rosen
YA™
New York

Published in 2020 by The Rosen Publishing Group, Inc.
29 East 21st Street, New York, NY 10010

Library of Congress Cataloging-in-Publication Data

Names: Pack, Erin, author. | Wolny, Philip, author.
Title: Everything you need to know about alcoholism / Erin Pack and Philip Wolny.
Description: New York : Rosen Publishing, 2020 | Series: The need to know library | Audience: Grade level 7–12. | Includes bibliographical references and index.
Identifiers: LCCN 2018054890| ISBN 9781508187493 (library bound) | ISBN 9781508187486 (pbk.)
Subjects: LCSH: Alcoholism—Juvenile literature. | Alcohol—Physiological effect—Juvenile literature.
Classification: LCC HV5066 .P33 2020 | DDC 362.292—dc23
LC record available at https://lccn.loc.gov/2018054890

Manufactured in the United States of America

CONTENTS

INTRODUCTION

When nature lovers visit national parks, they expect awe-inspiring scenery, adventure, and maybe to even learn a bit about the wilderness. In 2018, one tourist's vacation to Wyoming's Yellowstone National Park took an unnerving detour, however. His disruptive behavior not only got him into hot water with the authorities, but annoyed park visitors as well. He also put himself and others in danger.

It all started when fifty-five-year-old Oregon resident Raymond Reinke harassed a bison. A video circulated on YouTube of Reinke blocking traffic, taunting the bison, and making rude gestures. Cody, Wyoming's, *Cody Enterprise* newspaper reported in August 2018 that Reinke was "beating his chest like Tarzan while traffic was halted," confirming that he taunted the animal while cars swerved around him.

After his arrest, Reinke plead guilty to three counts of disturbing wildlife. A judge sentenced him to rehab for alcoholism, probation for disturbing the peace, and imposed several fines. But that wasn't the end of the story. Only a week later, he was arrested for another alcohol-related event in Glacier National Park, in neighboring Montana, and was sentenced to 130 days in jail and ordered to stay away from alcohol, including going into bars, for five years. He is officially banned from Yellowstone, Grand Teton, and Glacier National Parks as part of his probation.

The bison that are a popular attraction at Wyoming's Yellowstone National Park were harassed by a drunk Oregon man named Raymond Reinke in August 2018.

While Reinke's experience was unique, his struggles with alcohol abuse are alarmingly common. According to the National Institutes of Health (NIH), more than fifteen million Americans suffer from the various physical, mental, emotional, and financial consequences of alcoholism. There are minor ones, such as hangover headaches and fatigue, and severe ones, such as accidents from drunk driving, domestic and partner abuse, bankruptcy, as well as permanent ill health effects, including conditions such as cirrhosis, a disease that harms the human liver, and even kidney failure. The families of

One of the more negative behaviors associated with alcoholism is driving drunk, which can result in heavy fines or even jail time.

alcoholics, including spouses, partners, and children, as well as other family members and friends, coworkers, and neighbors can all suffer the effects of their alcohol abuse, too.

Alcoholism remains misunderstood. Some people don't believe they have a drinking problem, even when the evidence demonstrates otherwise. Similarly, many people around the world drink, but the majority are not alcoholics. Some alcoholics might drink while at work, school, or other inappropriate places.

Recognizing the warning signs of alcohol abuse is key to preventing it. When you recognize these signs, you can help your friends or family members with any struggles they might have with alcohol. You can also direct them to the many resources available for those who abuse alcohol to help them with recovery.

Educating yourself about the biological, psychological, and social impacts of alcoholism will help you learn how to spot an alcohol problem at any stage of its development. You also might be able to help the people in your life with drinking problems. You might even keep yourself from going down a dark road toward alcoholism.

CHAPTER ONE

WHAT IS ALCOHOLISM?

According to a 2017 *National Geographic* story, humans have been producing alcoholic beverages for at least nine thousand years. Many societies since have experienced the problems caused by alcohol abuse. William Gladstone, who served as British prime minister from 1868 to 1894, once noted that "alcoholism does more havoc than three historical scourges put together: famine, plague, and war."

The simplest definition of alcoholism is an addiction relating to the consumption of alcohol. Medical professionals also refer to alcoholism as alcohol use disorder, or AUD. Scientists describe it as a mental illness or as compulsive behavior resulting from a dependency on alcohol. Many alcoholics talk about their "need" to drink in order to cope with everyday life. Even when there are no positive effects from drinking, alcoholics will continue to drink.

WARNING SIGNS

For some people, the signs of alcoholism are noticeable. In others, however, they might be far from obvious. A person who enjoys drinking legally and responsibly occasionally is not considered to be an alcoholic. One of the first signs of alcoholism is not being able to limit how much alcohol one consumes. Another is drinking in secret. In many nations, drinking is seen as a social activity. When someone isolates himself while drinking, others may see this as a strong indication that he has an issue with alcohol.

Picture someone you know who seems to party a bit too much. According to the National Institute on Alcohol Abuse and Alcoholism (NIAAA), binge drinking can mean consuming as many as four drinks in one

ALCOHOLISM THROUGH THE AGES

Humans have enjoyed and abused alcohol since they discovered fermented fruit beverages. Fermentation is a chemical process used by makers of wines, beers, liquors, and other intoxicating beverages in which a fungus called yeast breaks down sugar to produce alcohol. Ancient civilizations from the Chinese to the ancient Greeks have all produced alcohol for recreation and rituals.

Alcohol abuse has been a problem throughout American history. Things got particularly bad in the late nineteenth and early twentieth centuries. Psychiatric institutions were often filled with alcoholics experiencing drinking-related psychoses, or severe mental health issues. Deaths due to liver failure were common. All of these problems led to various groups working to ban

(continued on the next page)

(continued from the previous page)

the production, import, sale, and distribution of alcohol entirely—a movement known as Prohibition.

Prohibition became the law of the land after its supporters forced lawmakers to make it an amendment to the US Constitution in January 1919. This banned the making, buying, and selling of alcohol throughout the entire United States from 1920 until 1933. Canada also had a similar period of alcohol prohibition in the early twentieth century.

Other countries around the world have had similar bans on alcohol, for either religious reasons or to curb social problems arising from drinking. According to the *CIA World Factbook*, alcohol is currently banned in nineteen countries, including Iran, Sri Lanka, parts of India, and Indonesia. In the past, countries that have legally banned alcohol include Norway, Finland, Yemen, and the Soviet Union.

Onlookers watch as barrels of illegal beer are destroyed and spilled into the sewers after being confiscated by law enforcement during the Prohibition era.

sitting for women and five for men. Heavy alcohol use is considered to be binge drinking five days or more in a month. One surefire sign of alcohol abuse is drinking to excess for most or all of the week.

A DOWNWARD SPIRAL

Heavy drinking two, three, or more times a week can easily become a spiral into daily alcohol abuse. A problem drinker might start getting blackout drunk, where he or she rarely or never remembers what happens to him or her after a certain amount of alcohol. A problem drinker often wakes up and can remember only hazy details or nothing at all. Such blackout drinking may become more frequent. It can be dangerous to the person and those around him or her.

A heavy drinker will also up his or her intake as his or her tolerance gets higher. Tolerance refers to the amount of alcohol any given person can handle without getting too drunk. A person new to drinking will have a fairly low tolerance. This means she needs very little to feel a buzz or actually get drunk—perhaps a can of beer or glass of wine will be enough. Frequent drinkers build their tolerance as they drink more and more. As with other drugs, like cocaine, the more users ingest, the more they need to get the same pleasurable feelings they once received from the activity. This process can continue until a person can barely get through the day without thinking about having a drink. Slurred speech while drinking is another telltale sign of alcohol abuse. So is a constant hangover—if someone drinks enough that every day there is a process of recovery, there is likely a problem with his or her consumption.

Alcohol abuse is a major driver of other social problems, including the drunk driving that results in many auto-related injuries and deaths annually. According to the Centers for Disease Control and Prevention (CDC), about one person dies from an alcohol-related traffic accident every fifty minutes in the United States. In addition, partner abuse and household financial troubles arise or are severely exacerbated when one or more partners drink heavily. The National Institutes of Health (NIH) reports that alcohol is the third leading cause of preventable death in the United States and Canada. Mothers Against Drunk

Mothers Against Drunk Driving (MADD) works to stop people, especially youth, from driving drunk. One of their main tactics is displaying demolished vehicles, like this one in Redondo Beach, California.

Driving (MADD), an organization that tries to minimize deaths from drunk driving, estimates that teen alcohol use kills more young people than all illegal drugs combined.

HOW MANY PEOPLE DOES ALCOHOLISM AFFECT?

For many people, the idea of alcoholism conjures up an image of a single, solitary person at a barstool or passed out on a street somewhere. Remember, however, that alcoholics have family who love them, jobs and coworkers, and have friends and others in their circle who can be severely affected by the secondary effects of alcoholism.

According to the NIAAA, more than 10 percent of children in the United States live with an alcoholic parent. Studies have also shown that adult nondrinkers who previously lived with heavy drinkers or alcoholics associated drinking with trauma, even years after initial incidents happen.

ROOT CAUSES OF A DISEASE

Alcoholism does not just happen on its own. Usually, a mixture of genetics and life experience (a combination of "nature and nurture") combine to create conditions for someone to fall under the influence of alcohol. According to the CDC, many alcoholics also suffer from various mental health conditions, such as depression and anxiety. These can be triggers for

Depression, anxiety, and other mental health issues, like dealing with severe trauma, can all be factors that can cause someone to choose alcohol as a form of self-medication.

alcohol abuse, especially if someone is unwilling or unable to seek help from mental health professionals and uses drinking to dull the pain of his or her experiences.

Trauma can also further trigger alcoholism. The Substance Abuse and Mental Health Services Administration (https://www.samhsa.gov) states that "individual trauma results from an event, series of events, or set of circumstances experienced by an individual as physically or emotionally harmful or life-threatening with lasting adverse effects on the individual's functioning and mental, physical, social, emotional, and spiritual well-being."

Some examples of trauma include physical and sexual abuse, child and partner abuse, the death of a friend or family member, a terrible accident like a car crash or surviving a disaster, and many other things that people need to cope with for the rest of their lives.

Major life events—like moving to a new town, going through the divorce of one's parents, coming out as LGBTQ+, or losing a close friendship—can all increase the chance that someone may turn to alcohol to cope with problems or will exacerbate a drinking habit she is already starting to develop.

Another common trigger for problem drinking can be tension at home, especially when a teen witnesses verbal or physical abuse.

AN ENDURING SOCIAL PROBLEM

Society can send very mixed signals about both alcohol and alcohol abuse. On the one hand, students will likely hear plenty of antialcohol lectures in school and be exposed to plenty of media warnings against alcohol abuse, peer pressure, and other phenomena associated with getting intoxicated.

On the other hand, advertising, marketing, and popular culture all constantly send the opposite messages: that drinking is cool, enjoyable, and something that popular and socially well-adjusted young people do.

This is usually the message that many teens get from their friends, classmates, and other peers. Teens don't need the internet or television to see alcohol all around them. From many of their own homes that are stocked with alcohol, to seeing others drinking while visiting a casual dining spot at the mall, to watching their peers drink, alcohol can seem to be everywhere.

In many places in the United States and Canada, alcohol is not difficult to get. This is even true for minors, or people under the legal drinking age. Drinking is seen as a socially acceptable way of winding down and relaxing. People use alcohol to socialize or to celebrate. In many cultures and communities, it is not uncommon to see alcohol used in religious ceremonies and services.

Alcohol is many things to many people. For adult drinkers of legal age, it is a source of relaxation and pleasure, something to enjoy on special occasions, or merely to celebrate the end of the workweek during a Friday happy hour. Parents take a drink as an end-of-day release from the sometimes stressful experience of raising kids. To others, however, alcohol and alcohol abuse are lurking threats hiding just around the corner, ready to swoop in and take control of their lives.

TEEN DRINKING

Peer pressure can certainly affect someone's decision to drink. This is especially true when teens are going through hormonal and life changes, learning the ropes when it comes to socializing, forming new friendships, and joining and leaving peer groups. It is difficult to pass up a drink if everyone else is doing it. Of course, underage drinking is against the law. In the United States, the legal drinking age is twenty-one. Anyone twenty-one and older can legally purchase alcohol in stores, bars and restaurants, and anywhere else it is sold. In addition, merchants and venues where alcohol is sold can get in trouble if they don't check ID, or card, potentially underage drinkers. They can face fines or even criminal prosecution if they sell alcohol to minors who later get intoxicated, end up driving drunk and hurt or kill others, or otherwise cause harm.

According to a May 2017 piece in MedPage Today, an online source of medical news, the CDC's Youth Risk Behavior Survey suggested that both alcohol consumption generally and binge drinking have declined in recent years among teenagers. From 1991 to 2015, the number of respondents to an extensive survey on teen drinking who said they had engaged in binge drinking in the past month fell from 31.3 percent to 17.7 percent. Nevertheless, as CDC researcher Marissa Esser stated in MedPage, "When we look at the trends, the reductions in the prevalence of current drinking and binge drinking would definitely be considered good news, but the other side of the coin is that one in three high school students still reported drinking alcohol, and more than half of these students were binge drinkers."

CHAPTER TWO

BECOMING AN ALCOHOLIC

The term "addictive personality" is used frequently when discussing drugs, binge eating, compulsive gambling, and other destructive habits. While having alcoholic parents or friends can certainly be a factor in a person starting to drink, the roots go deeper for some people. For many individuals, an addictive personality stems not just from their environment and upbringing, but also partly from genetics, especially when it comes to how our brains are wired.

Genetics is the study of inherited characteristics. If someone's family has several generations of alcoholics, he or she might develop a greater than average tendency to become an alcoholic, due to the genetic code passed down from family members to their descendants. Obviously, not everyone who has alcoholism in his or her family develops the disease. Instead, the genetic makeup of people with alcoholism in their families results in them having a higher likelihood of developing the disease. According to Recovery Village, a rehabilitation center for drug and alcohol abusers, children whose parents are alcoholics are four times

Other factors being equal, someone who has a family history of alcoholism may be more likely to abuse alcohol himself.

more likely to develop alcoholism later in life. They also quote widespread scientific findings that genetics might be responsible for as much as 50 percent of the risk involved with alcoholism.

THE EXCITING DEPRESSANT

Chemicals in the brain are where the mechanisms underlying alcohol abuse truly work. Alcohol acts as a chemical depressant. It tends to slow some biological processes down and relax the body and mind. This is true even though many people become aggressive, energized, and euphoric when they drink. This is because alcohol works on different parts of the brain differently. Some areas of the brain are depressed, or slowed down—including areas that handle rational thinking, keeping one's anger in check, and the ability to plan and execute actions and motions—while others are excited.

If someone is feeling happy overall, and then he or she has a drink and then another, that person will tend to feel more happy or positive. However, alcohol also amplifies other emotions, including negative ones, which may lead some people to get a reputation for being mean or hostile when drinking.

Eventually, when AUD becomes much worse, people drink increasing amounts of alcohol just to feel normal. When people drink too much alcohol, it triggers a shortage of the chemical dopamine, a neurotransmitter that helps move signals throughout the brain. Dopamine plays a major role in humans feeling happy and content.

Do alcoholics have different brains from the rest of the population? According to a 2008 article from *Psychology Today*, the shape of the brain of a heavy drinker is the same as that of a sober one, but the wiring is unusual. Another *Psychology Today* piece from 2016 details how researchers have identified the brain chemical dopamine as a key player in addiction. Dopamine is responsible for feelings of pleasure. Drinking (along with other drugs) tends to release more dopamine into the body. This buildup of dopamine makes getting buzzed from alcohol more difficult over weeks and months, especially if someone drinks heavily daily. The person craves more alcohol, or constant drinking, because the brain is demanding it of him or her.

THE DISEASE MODEL OF ADDICTION

In the past, alcoholism was treated as a character flaw or a moral failure. Although some people may still view AUD in this way, medical and mental health professionals nowadays view it as a disease, habit, or condition. As such, they view it as something that can be managed and controlled with the correct treatments and lifestyle changes. This way of viewing alcoholism is called the disease model of addiction.

The disease model views alcoholism and other addictions as a complex malfunctioning of the brain and body's many systems. According to the Addiction Center, an online portal run by the Beach House for Recovery, a for-profit rehabilitation center, the causes of alcohol use disorder are biological and must be treated like any other biological disease for the best treatment outcomes. It also means that alcohol use disorder isn't caused by just one reason. Instead, alcoholism can be caused by several different things at the same time.

Addiction can change the brain's limbic system, which controls emotions, behavior, and motivation. Like any other disease left untreated, alcoholism can lead to many physical and mental illnesses, such as tremors, seizures, or even death from liver failure, accidents, or brain damage.

PSYCHOLOGICAL CAUSES OF ALCOHOLISM

Trauma or psychological stress are also factors in whether someone turns to alcohol, whether for pleasure or to drink away the pain. Early trauma, such as parental abuse or the death of a sibling or caregiver, can contribute to someone's alcoholism later in life. People can also use alcohol as a coping mechanism in order to deal with psychological pain and stress happening in the present.

Frequent verbal and emotional abuse can cause severe psychological stress, or even trauma, and may lead a teen to make poor decisions when it comes to drinking.

A subset of mental illnesses called personality disorders sometimes accompany alcoholism. Whenever two or more mental illnesses or conditions occur at the same time, it is called comorbidity. It is not uncommon for an alcoholic to experience comorbidity with a personality disorder. Some personality disorders include antisocial personality disorder, borderline personality disorder, avoidant personality disorder, and dependent personality disorder. All have their own unique symptoms and causes. Not everyone who has these disorders will develop alcoholism. However, a failure to properly diagnose the conditions and symptoms arising from them can lead someone to embrace alcohol. Sufferers use alcohol as a way to self-medicate from problems they may not easily recognize.

TAKING A BREAK FROM ALL YOUR WORRIES

Teens with troubles at home or serious psychological issues are, sadly, natural candidates to be at risk for alcohol use disorder. But even high school students without these concerns are at risk and not just because of peer pressure. They must also handle school and any negative issues they encounter there, including bullying, academic struggles, and concerns about their future, as well as the stresses of the wider world.

Teens are also trying to carve out their own identities, and many tend to rebel against authority, whether that authority manifests itself in their parents, teachers,

Teen drinkers may find themselves waking up late for school, getting into trouble with the adults in their lives, and heading in a downward spiral that may lead to more drinking.

local law enforcement, or others in positions of power. Depression, anxiety, and other problems many youth experience can also feel overwhelming, even if they are not crippling or dangerous. With all this going on, many will look for an outlet that will let them have fun and blow off steam. Unlike grownups well into adulthood, their abilities to choose wisely, delay gratification, and negotiate a situation with a cool head are not nearly as well developed.

MYTHS AND FACTS

MYTH: Liquor is worse for drinkers than beer or wine.

FACT: The type of alcohol a person drink makes little difference. If too much is consumed, it can be dangerous.

MYTH: Alcohol is safer and more acceptable than other drugs.

FACT: Alcohol is one of the most destructive and addictive substances. In some ways, partly because it is more widespread, its social cost from medical problems, violence, abuse, and ruined lives make it as bad or even worse than many illegal substances, including hard drugs like cocaine or heroin.

MYTH: Alcohol is a stimulant and makes people more energetic.

FACT: Alcohol is a depressant. This means it makes your central nervous system slower and less reactive overall, even if some of its effects feel energizing.

CHAPTER THREE

WHEN DRINKING BECOMES A PROBLEM

Recognizing when occasional alcohol consumption becomes alcohol abuse and even full-blown alcoholism is the key to preventing someone from going down a dark path toward addiction. And like any addictive behavior, alcohol dependency can easily creep up slowly on the drinker.

THE LIFE OF THE PARTY

Many teens strive to be the center of attention in their clique, social group, or class. Both outgoing and shy youth can find themselves attracted to drinking because they feel it loosens them up and helps them become the life of the party. Every school or group may have one or more students or friends who go a little too far with their drinking to amuse their friends.

However, many party animals soon realize that there is a dark side to the good times. Rather than attracting others to their fun-loving ways, they may turn off many friends by being loud, belligerent, and stepping over the line in public. A few of the things an intoxicated teen might do to ruin any goodwill he or she has with friends and classmates include knocking things over, spilling drinks, being hard to talk to or starting arguments, being oversensitive and lashing out, or trying to start physical fights with others.

BUILDING TOLERANCE

Binge drinking is dangerous to begin with and makes up as much as 90 percent of all youth drinking, but not all binge drinkers develop a serious problem with alcohol. However, this type of drinking remains a dangerous gateway to alcoholism itself. One might start with one or two nights a week of binge drinking; maybe even just on weekend nights, like many people of all ages. Even feeling you have to drink to have fun is problematic. So is the idea that if there is alcohol around, you must partake to have a good time or fit in.

Imagine now that one or two nights slowly builds up to three or four nights. Before someone knows it, he has graduated to five or more nights a week. Someone who drinks every night for even a short while is in grave danger of addiction because he or she is building tolerance. Tolerance refers to the amount of alcohol someone can consume in one sitting to feel the same effect. When someone is new to drinking, a single light beer might get her pretty buzzed. Soon after, it takes two or three drinks to achieve the same feeling. Over time, a young person must consume large amounts to feel anywhere near as drunk as he or she used to.

Along the way, a drinker can expect to experience some bad hangovers. According to the Mayo Clinic, typical hangover symptoms "begin when your blood alcohol content (BAC) drops significantly and is at or near zero." They include many of the following, according to the clinic's website (https://www.mayoclinic.org):

- Fatigue and weakness
- Excessive thirst and dry mouth
- Headaches and muscle aches
- Nausea, vomiting, or stomach pain

Hangovers are one of the most unpleasant aspects of drinking. Imagine having a headache and feeling nauseated every day when you woke up.

- Poor or decreased sleep
- Increased sensitivity to light and sound
- Dizziness or a sense of the room spinning
- Shakiness
- Decreased ability to concentrate
- Mood disturbances, such as depression, anxiety, and irritability
- Rapid heartbeat

THE WARNING SIGNS PILE UP

One thing people who drink must carefully consider is just how much alcohol use is affecting their normal daily life. Binge-drinking teens might get too hungover to make it to classes, whether they are in high school or college. Coming in chronically late and eventually missing class altogether for long stretches of time might be a warning sign someone is losing control of his drinking.

Another telltale sign is a friend who loses interest in many of her hobbies or other pursuits. She may drop out of the computer club she loved so much, stop attending cheerleading practice, or simply seem less excited and involved in class than she used to be. It is important to stay vigilant if you fear that someone you know may be developing an alcohol problem and to make sure that another issue, such as a recent trauma or an unrelated medical or mental health issue, is not the cause of her behavior.

Other signs that arise as someone becomes dependent on alcohol are subtler and more psychological in nature. A person can hide the emotional toll of drinking for a long time. A person who was open and cheerful might become closed off and more secretive. The formerly easy-going friend who once greeted all conversation and questions with a smile might snap when questioned regarding his drinking. Previously gentle and kind people might even begin abusing loved ones, whether emotionally or even physically.

Getting angry or trying to change the subject are common reactions from sufferers of AUD. People with alcohol use disorder will prioritize drinking above loved

Someone who is drinking heavily might close himself off from other people, feeling isolated in his addiction. Other personality changes, like sudden fits of anger, might also take place.

ones, including family and close friends, and above pretty much every other part of their lives. Whenever alcohol becomes the emotional center of someone's world, the consequences can be fatal.

WHEN PROBLEMS ESCALATE

Typically, the most noticeable physical signs of an alcohol problem won't show up until late-stage alcoholism. A person's face can appear redder than normal because of burst blood vessels, typically on or around the nose and cheeks. Sudden weight gain or loss can also be a physical sign that alcoholism is a problem for someone. Serious memory loss, especially when followed by intense drinking binges, signals the need for medical intervention.

Frequent binge drinking, especially when it interferes in daily life and activities, can signal that a person depends on alcohol to function. If someone quits an activity he or she used to love in order to drink more, this is a sign of alcoholism. Other warning signs can include frequent mood swings, an inability to cope with problems unless drinking, a big change in behavior, and attempts to hide drinking.

STAGES OF ALCOHOL ABUSE

According to Alcohol.org, there are four main stages of alcoholism. Alcohol use disorder does not take over someone's life when he or she is sipping his or her first drink. Rather, addiction is a gradual process.

STAGE ONE: PREALCOHOLISM

During this stage, a person's drinking doesn't seem like a problem. In fact, it looks quite casual and not unusual for the person's age. Even close friends, parents, and other trusted adults likely cannot tell something is wrong with their loved one.

During prealcoholism, a person will drink to relieve mental stresses, cope with a tough situation, or to escape from reality on a regular basis. A prealcoholic will drink more and more and more frequently in order to get a buzz. The user begins to develop a tolerance for alcohol. Some other models of alcoholism that incorporate these four stages call this the early or adaptive stage of alcoholism.

STAGE TWO: EARLY ALCOHOLIC

This stage of alcoholism is marked by more extreme milestones and behaviors. The person will have experienced at least one blackout from drinking by this time. The sufferer might be torn between feeling guilty and ashamed and hoping to do something to stop his or her drinking and wanting to drink more. A teen might become obsessed with thoughts of drinking and plan his schedule around drinking more. Former boundaries—such as not drinking during school hours or with parents in the house—are crossed or set aside. It is very likely that the person will start to hide his drinking habits from family and friends at this stage. If someone is in school, he might start bringing hidden alcoholic beverages to school, while hiding evidence of his drinking with gum or other breath fresheners.

STAGE THREE: MIDDLE ALCOHOLIC

Drinkers at this stage might still want to help themselves and quit but have largely lost the ability to change their behavior.

People in the later stages of alcoholism constantly think about drinking, even during the few hours a day when they might be sober.

They continue to drink even as they see plainly that it is causing them major problems.

This stage, sometimes also known as the progression stage, is also when the physical signs of alcoholism become very noticeable. While during earlier stages, the drinker made an effort to hide her habits, she

When teens are drinking heavily, they lack the motivation to do much else and give little thought to the future. Getting their next drink is their sole priority.

now may start drinking at inappropriate times, even around teachers, relatives, and her boss. Because she does not want to risk being away from a comforting sip, the drinker will make sure she has a steady supply of alcohol at hand. She may drink in ways that are hazardous to herself and others, such as when driving, caring for children, or at work.

People at this stage of alcoholism might see their bodies start to change. Physical changes and symptoms can include weight gain and bloating. A reddening of the face, nose, and other parts of the body occurs for many people. Their breath might constantly smell of alcohol. The risk of bad withdrawal symptoms is strong at this point. Brittle hair and fingernails and a flushed, more leathery appearance might also be noticed on some drinkers. Since the drinker has stopped truly caring, she will stop eating properly. Her personal hygiene might suffer badly, too.

STAGE FOUR: LATE ALCOHOLIC

Late alcoholism, sometimes known as the conclusion stage, is marked by serious ill health effects. At this point, the drinker's life has completely unraveled or is about to. He drinks all day, every day, from morning through evening. Everything is now second to drinking, including friends, family, and work. Physical effects, such as cirrhosis or hardening of the liver, significant memory loss, and other symptoms become severe.

People at this stage need medical help to stop drinking. If they attempt to quit suddenly on their own, it could result in hallucinations, tremors, and even seizures in extreme cases. Some symptoms may even be life threatening, depending on how badly someone's body has already been ravaged. Liver damage will likely begin occurring at this stage, which can result in a yellowish color to the skin and eyes, a condition known as jaundice.

CHAPTER FOUR

GETTING HELP

Developing alcoholism is bad for your health and relationships. If the condition gets bad enough, complications begin to spiral out of control. According to the Mayo Clinic, some of the major complications of alcohol use disorder can include:

- Problems with other forms of substance abuse, including hard drugs like cocaine and heroin
- Relationship problems or abuse
- Legal problems arising from drunken behavior
- Increased likelihood of committing crimes or being the victim of a violent crime
- Participating in risky, unsafe sexual practices
- Increased risk of suicide
- Increased risk of accidental injuries, such as drowning and traffic accidents

"COLD TURKEY" AND WITHDRAWAL

One thing that lingers large in any drinker's and addict's mind is the fear of withdrawal. For late-stage alcoholics,

Alcoholics can get into trouble, including facing legal problems, because they can't control their actions or even remember what harmful things they've done while they were drinking.

withdrawal symptoms can be extremely severe. As with drugs like heroin, the physical symptoms of quitting drinking can be scary enough for the drinker to rational- ize his or her way out of even trying to stop. The pain of withdrawal, and even simply the idea of it, may seem worse than the terrible reality of full-blown alcoholism.

Mild withdrawal symptoms can appear within six hours of a person's last drink. These can include sweat- ing, sleeplessness or insomnia, nausea, vomiting, headaches, hands tremors, and nervousness and anx- iety. Add another six hours, and a heavy drinker may even experience hallucinations, hearing and seeing things that aren't there.

After two days or more, a small percentage of drinkers might get something known as delirium tremens, or DTs. DTs are characterized by fever, profuse sweating, shaking, heightened blood pressure and a racing heart, and confusion and sometimes accompanied by severe hallucinations and delusions.

Some people have the willpower and strength to stop drinking without any assistance whatsoever, otherwise known as "going cold turkey." It is certainly more feasible during the early stages of alcohol abuse but grows riskier the longer and more intensely someone has been abusing alcohol.

STAGING AN INTERVENTION

Friends worried about another friend's alcohol problem can stage an intervention, which is essentially a surprise meeting with the friend in need to convince him or her to seek help.

If you have a friend who is going down the dark road of addiction, email, text, or call a couple of mutual close friends to see if you can try to help the person in need. It is also important to contact family members, including siblings and parents, and to ask them respectfully to be part of the intervention, emphasizing the need to have as many people at the meeting as possible. Make sure that everyone who is part of the intervention shares the warning signs and symptoms they've witnessed.

It is also vital that everyone who attends the intervention agrees on concrete steps their addicted friend

In most rehab centers and other recovery environments, discussing your alcoholism and what led you to drink is an essential part of treatment.

or family member can take, even immediately after the meeting. Depending on how severe the problem is, drastic steps might be necessary. Someone at stage four may desperately need a referral to a detoxification program, otherwise popularly known as detox, and follow-up plans, including signing up for a stay at a rehabilitation center. Others might not be as ill and require only outpatient care. Look online at how several different organizations approach interventions, and contact local recovery organizations, nonprofits, government agencies, and religious organizations for help. Churches and other faith-based organizations are

THE CAGE QUESTIONNAIRE

If you suspect that you or a loved one might be abusing alcohol, the CAGE Questionnaire, a screening tool for problem drinking that was developed by Dr. John Ewing in 1970, can help you determine the extent of the problem. If a person answers yes to two or more of the CAGE questions, he or she should seek medical help for his or her drinking.

- Have you ever felt you should cut back on your drinking?
- Have people annoyed you by criticizing your drinking?
- Have you ever felt guilty about your drinking?
- Have you ever had a drink first thing in the morning to steady your nerves?

sometimes the only groups fighting drug and alcohol abuse in underserved and especially rural areas.

DETOX, REHAB, AND RECOVERY

There are several options for treating and controlling alcohol abuse. The first step, especially for someone hanging by a thread, is to get him or her to seek help. An early stage problem drinker may not need more than a visit to the doctor to start a plan of action to curb his or her behavior.

A late-stage alcohol abuser will be more difficult to convince. He or she may not come willingly, at first, but it is important to remember that one of the most important steps for any addict is to admit he or she has a problem. Without that admission, any detox or rehab may not have a lasting impact, and the drinker may simply go back to alcohol, a phenomenon known as relapse or relapsing. Regardless, the problem drinker will need to detox completely as a first step in his or her healing.

Detox is the process by which an addicted person rids his body of alcohol. As the liver begins to flush alcohol out of the body, withdrawal symptoms set in, often as quickly as six hours after he stops drinking. Withdrawal symptoms taper off after a week or two for most and are managed by a variety of prescription medications and other medical treatments. A serious detox should be handled by a doctor or other addiction professional who knows how to track a person's progress accurately.

Be aware that treatment for alcoholism is seldom completely without cost. Health insurance may coverage may pay for some or all of the cost of detox and treatment, but it depends on the plan. Some plans may not cover it at all. Careful research might be needed to find a place in your town, city, or county that provides discounted services to economically disadvantaged patients. Some facilities take payment on a sliding scale, which means you pay according to you or your family's wealth or income level. Free programs are also available if someone is caught up in the courts or juvenile justice system, especially as a result of alcohol-related charges. This group includes minors who have been arrested or detained for drunk driving, vandalism, fighting, or other infractions.

MEDICAL TREATMENTS

In the United States, the Food and Drug Administration (FDA) currently approves three medications to specifically treat alcoholism: disulfiram (also called Antabuse), naltrexone, and Campral. These medications are not meant to be used alone, but as part of a larger course of treatment, such as residential rehabilitation, therapy, or regular doctor visits. Drugs used to treat alcoholism work by making drinking an unpleasant experience for

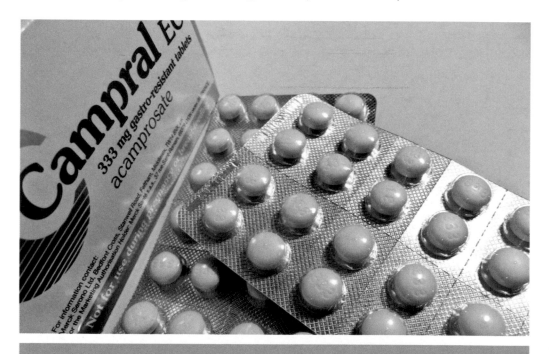

Acamprosate, sold under the Campral brand shown here, is used along with counseling and other treatment to prevent cravings and ease the symptoms of those who have quit drinking.

the alcoholic, either by removing the positive buzz or causing the person to vomit uncontrollably if he drinks while taking the medicine.

There are a myriad of drug and alcohol treatment centers in the United States and Canada. Many cities have several different options for alcoholics to find help. In residential treatment centers, people with alcohol use disorder receive medical treatment upon arrival and can stay for anywhere from one month to several months. Severe cases sometimes even require a year or more of help.

A typical stay at a rehab center will often include medication, detoxification, and basic physical assessments. After the initial medical assessments are completed, the patient will receive intensive psychological treatment to deal with the root of her addiction. These treatments can include medication, intense one-on-one therapy with mental health professionals, and group counseling.

EMOTIONAL AND PSYCHOLOGICAL SUPPORT

One of the most popular and enduring pillars of alcoholism treatment in North America is Alcoholics Anonymous—commonly known as AA. The organization was founded in 1935 in Akron, Ohio. AA is known for its Twelve Steps to Recovery. Group membership is free. Meetings are held in thousands of places worldwide and are often organized and facilitated by recovering alcoholics themselves.

Alcoholics Anonymous (AA), known for its Twelve Steps To Recovery, offers alcoholics places to meet for mutual support as they work their way through the program.

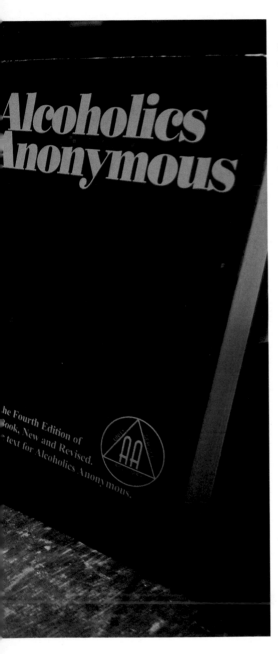

Typically, members of an AA group will work through the steps at their own pace and then report their progress or setbacks to the rest of the group. Meetings often take place once a week. In some cities, a recovering alcoholic can visit an AA meeting daily or even several times a day if need be. According to a 2016 report by the US surgeon general, AA and other twelve-step groups have been helpful for addicts largely because of the mutual support they offer.

Other individualized therapies and focused small group therapies have also been effective for alcoholics. Such treatments help alcoholics discover the psychological reasons that might have been causing them to drink to excess, how to deal with past traumas, and tips they can use to prevent relapse, which means falling back into alcohol use disorder after a period of significant improvement.

Family members and friends of alcoholics can also go to support groups. Some of these groups are often offshoots of AA, including Alateen, which is aimed toward young people who have been impacted by a loved one's drinking. Local counselors and other mental health care professionals can usually steer those in need to these support groups. As with AA, many meetings happen in school or church settings, where space and other resources are often donated.

DUAL-ADDICTION TREATMENT

Many alcoholics also deal with addictions to other drugs as well as alcohol. This is called dual addiction. According to the NIH, the most common dual addiction drug cases in North America come from opioids like fentanyl, as well as heroin.

Alcoholism is dangerous on its own. Combined with the abuse of other drugs, it can be even more devastating. Dual-addiction treatment requires more medical intervention than solely treating alcoholism. These treatment programs need to recognize both the drug and alcohol issues present in the addict and work to treat both issues at the same time so the person can start down the road to recovery.

CHAPTER FIVE

CHOOSING LIFE, STAYING CLEAN

Alcoholics who seek and maintain treatment can lead successful, fulfilling lives. Sarah Hepola, a New York resident, was interviewed by the United Kingdom's *Telegraph* newspaper in 2015. Hepola's drinking problem began at age eleven. She became sober at age thirty-five. "I couldn't drink like normal people," Hepola explained. "My craving was so ferocious I couldn't control it." She drank more and more, almost burning down her apartment after a long night of drinking and blacking out. Finally, Hepola's therapist said, "I can't help you unless you stop drinking." Now, Hepola has been sober for almost five years. "My life is so good, so it's easy not to drink."

Although Hepola's story is harrowing, it isn't unusual. Many alcoholics hit what is called rock bottom, or the lowest, most embarrassing point of their disease, which causes them to consider getting treatment. This moment of clarity is often met with the willingness to recover from alcohol use disorder.

NEVER GIVE UP

Even for late-stage alcoholism, there is still hope. Recovery is always possible. According to a July 2013 article in the *Bangor Daily News*, addicts make the best addiction counselors. Whether as professional mental health workers or informal leaders in groups like AA, alcoholics in recovery can speak from their own experiences. Sometimes, recovery takes more than one attempt. An alcoholic must truly desire recovery because it is a commitment to put oneself through the mentally and potentially physically painful ordeal of quitting drinking.

MANAGING ALCOHOLISM: ONE SUCCESS STORY FROM HOLLYWOOD

Even though he's been sober for almost twenty years, actor Robert Downey Jr. still calls himself an alcoholic. When speaking about his dual addiction to drugs and alcohol to *Vanity Fair* magazine, he said: "Job one is get out of that cave. A lot of people do get out but don't change. So the thing is to get out and recognize the significance of that aggressive denial of your fate, come through the crucible forged into a stronger metal."

Downey hit rock bottom in 1996 after years of drug and alcohol abuse. One summer night, he was so intoxicated he wandered out of his Los Angeles apartment in just his underwear, broke into a neighbor's house (he later told others he believed it was his own home), and passed out in a child's bedroom.

Many people still refer to themselves as alcoholics, even when they haven't had a sip of alcohol in decades. They do this because recovering from alcohol use disorder can be a delicate process, one that requires constant focus and intention. How do alcoholics manage such an intense disease? Most abstain from alcohol completely. This means they cannot have just one glass of champagne on New Year's Eve, drink wine at a religious service, or just have a beer while watching a football game.

Managing alcoholism also means being mindful about how recovering alcoholics spend their time, including where they socialize. Many will not go into a bar, in order to avoid even the slightest temptation of a drink. Others will not be around other people who are heavily drinking.

Although the journey can be frustrating, recovering alcoholics are happy to work hard to avoid a relapse. According to Robert Downey Jr., sobriety is worth fighting for.

Alcoholics in recovery are in a unique position to help others. They have been through difficult experiences and have lived to tell their stories. They are also more likely to have empathy for other recovering addicts because they might have hit rock bottom themselves. Conversely, alcohol abusers in need will be more willing to trust those who understand what it's like to be addicted to alcohol.

HOPE ON THE HORIZON

New therapies and treatments are on the horizon for alcoholics. According to the NIH's National Institute on Alcohol Abuse and Alcoholism (NIAAA), new psychological treatments such as motivational enhancement therapy (MET) can be helpful for people dealing with alcohol use disorder. MET uses four sessions or meet-ups to interview patients and help them come to their own conclusions about the best possible course of treatment. Medication and therapy combined seems to be the ideal course of action for many recovering

One-on-one counseling is another major part of rehab programs. For many people, it is as important a part of their recovery as group work and prescription medication.

alcoholics. Since alcohol use disorder impacts 16.6 million Americans per year, effective medications will certainly be in strong demand.

There are new research breakthroughs and discoveries in addiction studies happening all the time. As ideas about the disease model of addiction continue to evolve, there is reason to believe a new breakthrough is just around the corner. According to Dr. Ting-Kai Li, the former director of the NIAAA, most

A vital component of defeating your addiction is spending time doing activities that you love with people who support your recovery.

people are able to recover from alcohol use disorder.

Although alcohol use disorder can be tough on a person's body and mind, the disease can be overcome with the proper support and treatment methods. Recovery looks different for different people, so two people's paths to wellness may have little in common besides the desired destination. There is no straight line to success, and this includes success in recovery. But there is hope for people who must deal with their potentially deadly addiction to alcohol.

10 GREAT QUESTIONS TO ASK AN ADDICTION COUNSELOR

If you or a loved one is dealing with alcoholism, here are ten starter questions to ask an addiction counselor:

1. How can alcoholism impact a drinker's life and overall health?
2. What is the best way to help a friend or relative treat his or her alcoholism?
3. What can I do if I think someone I know might be an alcoholic?
4. Can alcoholism cause physical problems and symptoms?
5. Are there special medications used to treat alcohol abuse?
6. When should someone be alarmed by a drinking problem?
7. What can my friend do to keep his or her drinking in control?
8. What are the stages of alcoholism?
9. What are alternatives to drinking that are fulfilling and positive?
10. Are medical or psychological treatments more effective for alcoholism?

GLOSSARY

alcohol use disorder The medical diagnosis for problem drinking that has become severe.

binge drinking Drinking four or more beverages in a single sitting.

blood alcohol content The measurement of alcohol in one's system, used by medical and law enforcement professionals to determine whether someone is intoxicated.

comorbidity The presence of two or more chronic diseases or conditions in the same patient, such as alcoholism with a diagnosed personality disorder.

complication Something that makes a situation more difficult to deal with.

delirium tremens A severe side effect of alcohol withdrawal, occurring within about forty-eight hours of giving up drinking that includes symptoms such as hallucinations and tremors.

depressant A drug or other substance that slows down the workings of the nervous system.

detox The immediate cleansing of alcohol out of one's system when someone is first attempting to get sober, it can also refer to the facility where this process takes place.

diagnose To identify an illness or condition.

empathy The ability to understand and have compassion for another person's feelings and experiences.

fermentation A chemical process that turns food sugar into alcohol.

harrowing Frightening or alarming.

moment of clarity A particular moment or milestone that makes a person realize something profound about his or her life.

Prohibition The era from 1919 to 1933 in the United States when alcohol was severely restricted in the nation. The term also refers to the law passed via constitutional amendment to ban alcohol in 1919.

rehab Short for rehabilitation, which refers to any program or facility that helps someone recover from addiction.

sobriety The state of being free of alcohol and drugs.

tolerance The ability to consume increasing amounts of alcohol without the same effects.

trauma A life-changing event that often has a negative impact on the sufferer.

withdrawal The difficult process of quitting drinking or drug use, often accompanied by severe physical symptoms and emotional hardship.

FOR MORE INFORMATION

Alcoholics Anonymous (AA)
475 Riverside Drive, 11th Floor
New York, NY 10115
Website: https://www.aa.org
Facebook: @1StepAtTheTime
Twitter: @AlcoholicsAA
Alcoholics Anonymous, founded in 1939, is a nonprofit
  organization dedicated to helping alcoholics and recovering alcoholics who are seeking a lifetime of sobriety. It is one of the largest recovery organizations
  in the world, providing meetings, support groups,
  and other resources for recovering alcoholics.

Canadian Centre on Substance Use and Addiction
  (CCSA)
75 Albert Street, Suite 500
Ottawa, ON K1P 5E7
Canada
(833) 235-4048
Website: http://www.ccdus.ca/eng/Pages/default.aspx
Twitter: @CCSAcanada
This organization was created by Parliament with the
  aim of providing national leadership on issues re-
  lated to substance abuse. CCSA also runs several
  substance abuse and addiction centers.

Canadian Society on Addiction Medicine (CSAM)
1444 40th Street SW
Calgary AB T3C 1W7

Canada
(403) 246-9393
Website: https://www.csam-smca.org
Facebook: @canadiansocietyofaddictionmedicine
Twitter: @csam_smca
CSAM centers their efforts on developing new drugs
    and treatments that will potentially offer medical
    solutions to addictions and also serves to represent
    medical professionals who treat patients dealing
    with addiction issues.

Center for the Study of Addictions and Recovery (CSTAR)
71 West 23rd Street, 4th Floor
New York, NY 10010
(212) 845-4400
Website: http://www.ndri.org/cstar.html
CSTAR is dedicated to researching the links between
    brain chemistry, psychology, and addiction.

National Council on Alcoholism and Drug Dependence
217 Broadway, Suite 712
New York, NY 10007
(212) 269-7797
Website: https://www.ncadd.org
Facebook and Twitter: @NCADDNational
This seventy-year old organization provides a wealth
    of resources and information about alcoholism
    and drug dependence, with the primary goal of
    helping individuals and their families succeed in
    long-term recovery.

National Institute of Mental Health (NIMH)
6001 Executive Boulevard, Room 6200
MSC 9663
Bethesda, MD 20892
(866) 615-6464
Website: https://www.nimh.nih.gov
Facebook and Twitter: @nimhgov
This research organization undertakes studies and re-
    leases papers on addiction, dual diagnosis, and the
    connections between alcoholism and mental health.

National Institute on Alcohol Abuse and Alcoholism
    (NIAAA)
5635 Fishers Lane, MSC 9304
Bethesda, MD 20892-9304
(866) 615-6464
Website: https://www.niaaa.nih.gov
Instagram and Twitter: @niaaanews
A part of the larger National Institutes of Health
    (NIH), the NIAAA provides a wealth of information
    for those dealing with alcohol abuse and under-
    takes cutting-edge research studying addiction
    and recovery.

FOR FURTHER READING

Abramowitz, Melissa. *Understanding Addiction.* San Diego, CA: ReferencePoint Press, 2018.

Brezina, Corona. *Alcohol and Drug Offenses: Your Legal Rights.* New York, NY: Rosen Publishing, 2015.

Etingoff, Kim. *Drugs and Alcohol.* Broomall, PA: Mason Crest, 2015.

Henneberg, Susan. *Defeating Addiction and Alcoholism.* New York, NY: Rosen Publishing, 2016.

Landau, Jennifer. *Helping a Friend with an Alcohol Problem.* New York, NY: Rosen Publishing, 2017.

Meyer, Terry Teague. *I Have an Alcoholic Parent. Now What?* New York, NY: Rosen Publishing, 2015.

Newell, Ella. *The Hidden Story of Alcoholism.* London, UK: Raintree, 2016.

Parks, Peggy J. *The Dangers of Alcohol.* San Diego, CA: ReferencePoint Press, 2017.

Poole, Hilary W. *Drug and Alcohol Dependence.* Broomall, PA: Mason Crest, 2016.

Spilsbury, Louise. *Drinking and Drugs? Skills to Avoid 'Em and Stay Cool.* New York, NY: Enslow Publishing, 2019.

BIBLIOGRAPHY

Boyles, Salynn. "Teen Drinking Rates Continue to Decline." Medpage Today, May 11, 2017. https://www.medpagetoday.com/publichealthpolicy/publichealth/65228.

Centers for Disease Control and Prevention. "Impaired Driving. Get the Facts." Retrieved November 16, 2018. https://www.cdc.gov/motorvehiclesafety/impaired_driving/impaired-drv_factsheet.html.

Central Intelligence Agency. *The World Factbook, 2013–2014*. Washington, DC, 2013.

Cohen, Rich. "The Ride of His Life." *Vanity Fair*, September 23, 2014.

Curry, Andrew. "Our 9,000-Year Love Affair with Booze." *National Geographic*, February 2017. https://www.nationalgeographic.com/magazine/2017/02/alcohol-discovery-addiction-booze-human-culture.

Dasgupta, Amitava. *The Science of Drinking: How Alcohol Affects Your Body and Mind*. Lanham, MD: Rowman and Littlefield Publishers, 2012.

Dovey, Dana. "Alcohol Addiction Affects Dopamine Levels in Brain, Making It Harder to Catch a Buzz, Easier to Relapse." Medical Daily, March 4, 2016. https://www.medicaldaily.com/alcohol-addiction-dopamine-levels-376577.

Dudley, Robert. *The Drunken Monkey: Why We Drink and Abuse Alcohol*. Berkeley, CA: University of California Press, 2014.

Freedman, Lew. "Jail for Bison Taunter." *Cody Enterprise*, August, 27, 2018. http://www.codyenterprise.com.

Gaitley, Iain. *Drink: A Cultural History of Alcohol.* New York, NY: Gotham Books, 2009.

LaPierre, Jim. "Hope for the Late Stage Alcoholic." *Bangor Daily News*/Recovery Rocks, July 27, 2013. http://recoveryrocks.bangordailynews.com/2013 /07/27/addiction/cumulative-recovery-offers-hope-for -the-late-stage-alcoholic.

Leonard, Kimberly. "Teen Drinking Continues to Decline in the U.S." *U.S. News & World Report*, December 16, 2014. https://www.usnews.com/news/blogs/data -mine/2014/12/16/teen-drinking-continues-to-decline -in-the-us.

Mayo Clinic. "Hangovers." Retrieved November 8, 2018. https://www.mayoclinic.org/diseases-conditions /hangovers/symptoms-causes/syc-20373012.

Narconon Arrowhead. "History of Alcoholism." Retrieved November 7, 2018. https://www.narcononarrowhead .org/addiction/alcohol/history-of-alcoholism.html.

National Institutes of Health (NIH)/National Institute on Alcohol Abuse and Alcoholism (NIAAA). "Alcohol Use Disorder." Retrieved November 8, 2018. https:// www.niaaa.nih.gov/alcohol-health/overview-alcohol -consumption/alcohol-use-disorders.

National Institutes of Health (NIH)/National Institute on Alcohol Abuse and Alcoholism. "Drinking Levels De-fined." Retrieved November 4, 2018. https://www .niaaa.nih.gov/alcohol-health/overview-alcohol -consumption/moderate-binge-drinking.

National Institutes of Health (NIH)/National Institute on Alcohol Abuse and Alcoholism (NIAAA). "NIH Be-gins Clinical Trial of New Medication for Alcohol Use Disorder." Press Release, June 25, 2015.

Nordqvist, Christian. "What Is Alcohol Abuse Disorder, and What Is the Treatment." Medical News Today, May 29, 2018. https://www.medicalnewstoday.com /articles/157163.php.

O'Connor, Lynn E. "Brains Wired for Addiction (No Kidding) and What This Says About 'Harm Reduction'." *Psychology Today,* February 28, 2012.

Pierucki, Heather. "Why Is Acohol so Addictive?" Drugabuse.com. Retrieved November 2, 2018. https://drugabuse.com/library/alcohol-addiction.

Russell, Scarlett. "Drinking by 11, Alcoholic by 20, Sober by 35; One Woman's Story." *Telegraph*, June 27, 2015. https://www.telegraph.co.uk/women /womens-health/11693738/Drinking-by-11 -alcoholic-by-20-sober-by-35-one-womε   ry .html.

Webmd.com. "What Is Alcohol Withdra'   trieved November 5, 2018. https://www.w   m/mental -health/addiction/alcohol-withdr   ptoms -treatments#1.

Western Oklahoma State Co'   onolism - Myths vs. Facts." Retrieved N   , 2018. https:// www.wosc.edu/ind   ε=counseling -alcoholism-myths-vs-racts.

INDEX

A

addiction, 8, 20, 21, 26–27, 32, 38, 41, 43, 46, 48, 51, 52
addictive personality, 18
admission, 41
advertisement, 15
Alcoholics Anonymous (AA), 43, 45–46, 48
alcohol use disorder, 8, 21, 23, 30–31, 36, 43, 46, 47, 49, 50–51
anxiety, 13, 24, 29, 37

B

ban, 4, 9–10
behavior, 4, 8, 17, 21, 26, 29, 31–33, 36, 40
binge drinking, 9, 11, 17, 27, 29, 31
blackout drunk, 11, 32, 47
blood alcohol content, 28
buzz, 11, 21, 27, 32, 43

C

CAGE Questionnaire, 40
cirrhosis, 5, 35
cold turkey, 36, 38
comorbidity, 23
complication, 36

coping mechanism, 22
counseling, 43

D

delirium tremens, 38
dependence, 8, 23, 26, 30–31
depressant, 19, 25
depression, 13, 24, 29
detox, 39–41, 43
diagnosis, 23
disease model, 13, 18, 21, 47, 49, 51
dopamine, 20
drunk driving, 5, 12, 13, 17, 34, 42
dual addiction, 46, 48

E

empathy, 49

F

fatigue, 5, 28
fermentation, 9

G

genetics, 13, 18–19
Gladstone, William, 8

ABOUT THE AUTHORS

Erin Pack holds a BA in history and a master's degree in social studies education from the University of North Texas. She has taught high school social studies and debate for several years and is currently studying to become a school psychologist. She has previously written mental health information books for Rosen and lives with her family in Utah.

Philip Wolny is an editor and author born in Poland and raised in New York City. He has written numerous informational and self-help books for youth, many covering health and wellness issues. Some of his works for Rosen Publishing include *Syphilis* (Your Sexual Health), *I Have an STD. Now What?* (Teen Life 411), *Abusing Prescription Drugs*, and *The Truth About Heroin* (Drugs & Consequences), among others. He hopes that everyone reading about addiction comes to the topic open-minded and internalizes the compassion and sympathy many of our friends, neighbors, and family members need. He lives in Queens, New York, with his wife and daughter.

PHOTO CREDITS

Cover urbazon/E+/Getty Images; back cover photo by Marianna Armata/Moment/Getty Images; p. 5 William Campbell/Corbis News/Getty Images; p. 6 George Steinmetz/Corbis Documentary/Getty Images; pp. 8, 18, 26, 36, 47 dusanpetkovic/iStock/Getty Images; p. 10 Hulton Archive/Getty Images; p. 12 prettyfoto/Alamy Stock Photo; pp. 14, 30 Monkey Business Images/Shutterstock.com; p. 15 Nancy Ney/Photodisc/Getty Images; p. 19 Maskot/Getty Images; p. 22 Joel Sartore/National Geographic/Getty Images; p. 24 RyanJLane/E+/Getty Images; p. 28 © iStockphoto.com/fizkes; p. 33 BonNontawat/Shutterstock.com; p. 34 John Wollwerth/Shutterstock.com; p. 37 ImagesbyTrista/iStock/Getty Images; p. 39 Photographee.eu/Shutterstock.com; p. 42 Stuart Aylmer/Alamy Stock Photo; pp. 44–45 John van Hasselt/Corbis Historical/Getty Images; p. 50 asiseeit/E+/Getty Images; p. 51 Antonio Guillem/Shutterstock.com.

Design: Michael Moy; Layout: Tahara Anderson; Editor: Jennifer Landau; Photo Researcher: Bruce Donnola